# KNOSSOS

## THE PALACE OF MINOS
### WITH ITS DEPENDENT BUILNDINGS

## THE MINOAN CIVILIZATION
### AND
## THE MUSEUM OF HERAKLION

Mythology - Archaeology - Excavations
Explanatory text of map

by
**CHRISTOS Z. MATHIOULAKIS**

SKETCHES: N. GOUVOUSSIS

Minos

ATHENS, 1974

Arthur J. Evans

# PROLOGUE

By Dr. PETER WARREN

Archaeologist Sub-Manager, English
School of Archaeology of Athens

Mr Christos Mathioulakis has written a new and fascinating Guide to the Minoan civilization and the palace of Knossos. The author is himself a Cretan and his work is of unusual interest in that it expresses a Cretan viewpoint, an islander's understanding of the daily life and thoughts of his fellow islanders over three thousand three hundred years ago. The first part of the Guide is a sympathetic appreciation of the Minoans and their unique achievements in art, building, religion, trade writing. The book thus explains the real Bronze Age, Minoan background to some of the most entertaining legends and stories of Classical Greece. In addition, Mr. Mathioulakis's historical account takes in the latest views of archaeologists based on excavations in Crete and outside it, for example the recent work of Professor Platon in the new Palace of Kato Zakro and of Professor Marinatos on the volcanic island of Santorini, where an amazing Bronze Age settlement, perhaps a Minoan colony, is coming to light beneath the pumice and lava.

The second section of the book guides the visitor round the palace of Minos, emphasising the most intriguing parts of the building; an account of the great Archaeological Museum of Heraklion follows, with reference o some of the best known finds of the Minoan civilization.

Included with the Guide is a wonderful isometric drawing of the reconstructed Palace at Knossos. Here one can obtain a unique picture of the great building as it must have looked in its hey-day, storey upon storey, with brightly coloured architectural detail, the whole surrounded by noble dependent buildings amid verdant gardens. Mr. Mathioulakis's accurate visual reconstruction will certainly provide visitors with that much sought whole impression of the Palace as they explore for themselves the evidenc which has survived in the labyrinthine passages and rooms brought to ligh by Sir Arthur Evans. Most appropriately Mr Mathioulakis's Guide is in scribed to the memory of that great archaeologist and scholar.

Dr. PETER WARREN

Archaeologist

*Rhyton of steatite form of a bullhead*

## TO THE MEMORY OF SIR ARTHUR EVANS (1851 - 1941)

Explorer of Knossos. A wealthy Englishman, son of an industrialist and antiquarian, he was educated at Harrow School, and the Universities of Oxford and Göttingen. He devoted himself passionately to the study of archaeology and anthropology. He travelled to Finland and Lapland, and the Balkans. On one of these journeys he felt an urge to explore ancient civilizations and in 1883 visited Mycenae.

ARTHUR EVANS

Like Schliemann he became puzzled by the problem of the origin of the Mycenaean civilization. He too believed that for this he must turn to the island of Crete. From the year 1894 he explored, and carried out a small excavation at Aghios Onouphrios in the plain of Messara. But he was hindered from continuing his explorations by the events which were then stirring in the island. The proclamation of the autonomy of Crete in 1898 resulted in his being able to undertake excavations at Knossos, with the assistance of DUNCAN MACKENZIE. He discovered the great P a l a c e  o f  M i n o s, the L i t t l e  P a l a c e, the R o y a l  V i l l a, the T e m p l e  T o m b, the C a r a v a n s e r a i, where guests from the south first stopped before entering the palace, the H o u s e  o f  t h e  H i g h  P r i e s t, the C e m e t e r y  o f  Z a p h e r  P a p o u r a, and that of I s o p a t a, as well as the harbour of K o m o, from which the Cretan ships sailed away for Egypt and Libya. He also discovered and explored the Minoan route from Komo to Knossos.

The publication of his memorable work on Knossos serves now as the basis for the study of ancient Crete (1).

(1) Sir Arthur Evans, The Palace of Minos at Knossos. Vols. I-IV, 1921-35. Index, Volume, Evans and J.E.A. Evans, 1936.

But Evans did not stop here. Using concrete he reconstructed the ancient monuments by joining the fallen parts, restored the paintings and sculptures and, from the ruins and rubble which he had unearthed, he gave back to the Palace her ancient appearance.

The discovery of the Palace of Minos at Knossos is one of the most noteworthy events in our century. Evans offered himself and his fortune, and by his efforts, he managed to render not only to Greece but to all humanity a great service. The reconstruction and erection of certain sections of the palace in their initial form must have been due to an inspiration inborn in Evans and certainly resulted in a rebirth of a wonderful civilization which had been considered to form part of Greek Mythology. Had it not been for Evans the palace might have stayed as a shapeless and lifeless pile of rubble. It was he who gave those dubious ruins not only their form but also their very soul...

Imagination is a primary element and condition for the success of any venture. Evans had been favoured fully with the imaginative powers precedent to success. Imagination was very highly developed in him; the long time he spent on his quest was an effort exerted with full confidence in success. He had the feeling that his objective could be achieved; that feeling caused him to put in a continuous, intense activity which was sustained and grew with the successes which came as the work progressed. His imagination must have made him count himself as being one of the Minoans of that ancient era. His intelligence matched his imagination too. Thus, he came to conceive the past faithfully, caught vividly the event, no matter how complicated that might have been, studied and cherished all the repercussions and then sat down and lovingly transmitted his findings. This indeed was the great objective of Evans – an invincible urge to save from oblivion and ignorance every beautiful form, figure or shape.

It is to him that we owe so much because he drew the attention of the world to the Pre-Hellenic civilization of the island of Crete and because he offered his successors a free field most suitable for a deeper exploration of the Minoan era. A new civilization emerges therefrom before the eyes of archaeologists and that civilization illuminates the initial stages of the ancient Hellenic World.

We owe it to Evans that we must no longer consider King Minos as a simply legendary figure. The island with the 'hundred cities' which Homer sang of became not only the creation of a poet, but also a historic reality.

These great services of Evans made him famous throughout the world and in 1911 Great Britain knighted him, Sir Arthur Evans.

In honour of his great services to humanity and in everlasting memory of him, the bust of Arthur Evans has been placed on the southern side of the West Court of the palace of Knossos.

To the west of the palace lies the 'Villa Ariadne,' built in 1906 and used by Evans as his working premises. Tourists and visitors visit the villa in token of reverence for the man.

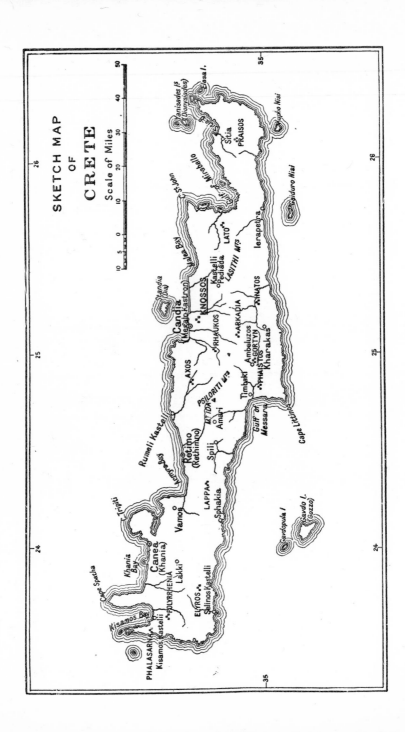

SKETCH MAP

OF

CRETE

Scale of Miles

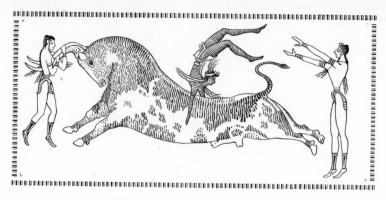

*Bullfight – Wall painting (Museum)*

## PREFACE

«Κρήτη τις γαῖ στί, μέσῳ ἐνὶ οἴνοπι πόντῳ, καλὴ καὶ πίειρα, πε
ρίρρυτος· ἐν δι᾽ ἄνθρωποι πολλοὶ ἀπειρέσιοι, καὶ ἐννήκοντα πόληες—
ἄλλη δ᾽ ἄλλων γλῶσσα μεμιγμένη· ἐν μὲν 'Αχαιοί, ἐν δ᾽ 'Ετεόκριτες
μεγαλήτορες, ἐν δὲ Κύδωνες, Δωριέες τε Τριχάϊκες διά τε Πελασγοί —
τῆσι δ᾽ ἐνὶ Κνωσός, μεγάλη πόλις· ἔνθε τε Μίνως ἐννέωρος βασίλευε
Διὸς μεγάλου· ὀαριστής, πατρὸς ὁμοῖο πατήρ, μεγαλοθύμου Δευκαλίω-
νος, Δευκαλίων δ᾽ ἐμὲ τίκτε καὶ 'Ιδομενῆα ἄνακτα...».

(HOMERE ODYSSEE Τ 172-180)

*As is well known, the island of Crete, this nymph of the Mediter-
ranean Sea, exercises on the visitor a peculiar and most subtle attraction
through the unique Minoan civilization which thrived on it. Nowhere else
can one feel so intensely the imposing presence of History as in this southern island of the Greek area and this feeling is further enhanced by
its excellent climate ;*

*To all of which should be added also the peculiar mode of life there,
the topical colour as well as the heroic tradition of its inhabitants.*

*It is not difficult for the visitor to the island of Crete to come to the
conclusion that, for geopolitical reasons, it was most natural for the
island to have constituted in ancient times a self-sustained geographic
and economic unit, as it indeed from the very first. All favourable
conditions amply existed here for the evolution in the island of an
easy and comfortable life, so that by-and-by a most remarkable civi-
lizarion could develop. It must have been a most temperate climate ;
the choice products of the Cretan soil, the particularly flexible, affable
and sensitive character of the Minoan race which, altogether, finished by*

9

generating a physical offspring – the wonderful and joyful Cretan civilization – so crowded with impressiv events and so distinguished by its intensity and its lavishness in the pursuit of the enjoyment of life.

Archaeological researh started to reveal to us from the beginning of this century this startling civilization.

We now hear of the "P a x  M i n o i c a" indeed no other people living in ancient times in the Greek area was ever able to boast of that unity and peace which the Cretans of the Minoan era succeeded in attaining.

It was the Cretans themselves who first tasted this unity and peace ; under it they developed a civilization which was both refined and idyllic It is exactly this civilization which their art reflects, for example, in their fabulous and grandiose palace of Minos and it is this palace which we present in our present work in all its architectural splendour ; the archaeological excavations give us the assurance that it is here reproduced exactly as it most probably was during the Minoan era.

We have based our work on the researches of the great English archaeologist, scientist and explorer Sir Arthur Evans, as well as others, namely R.W. Hutchinson, Fr. Schachermeyr, J.W. Graham, Raymond Matton and J.D.S. Pendlebury.

We also owe much to the works of many eminent Greek archaeologists. We believe we have succeeded in making it possible for the visitor to the palace of Minos and for the student of the Minoan civilization to grasp the picture of that great historical era as well as the splendours of its architecture.

We are certain that we are offering a popularized but at the same time a scientifically well based work to the foreign visitor and to the Greek tourist and, more generally, to G r e e k  T o u r i s m.

CHRIS.  MATHIOULAKIS

*The Throne of Minos (Palace of Knossos)*

# KNOSSOS

## THE PALACE OF MINOS

The mighty palace of King Minos lies south of Heraklion at a distance of five kilometres. It stands on the hill known as Kephala, above the banks of the river Kairatos and surrounded by olive trees, vineyards and cypresses.

Throughout the ages this palace stood as a most peculiar and intricate building ; it was indeed a l a b y r i n t h, such as our imagination might have conceived when we were children. It is not strange that with the lapse of time it came to be considered as a legend.

By-and-by, too, archaeological research has counted for ancient Crete ιot merely ninety, as Homer sang, but more than one hundred cities.

As far back as four thousand years ago three of these cities – K n o s- s o s, P h a i s t o s and M a l l i a – were especially distinguished ; all three of them thrived during the ascendency in Crete of the great Minoan civilization.

In her turn, from among these three cities, it was K n o s s o s which became more particularly pre-eminent. Knossos, the capital of the strong and legendary King Minos, was one of the greatest cities of the ancient world. Her population was in the range of 100,000. She formed one of the earliest and largest settlements of the neolithic era and grew up to a surprising grandeur and beauty during a succession of three historical epochs of the Minoan civilization.

Basing his conclusions on the strata which he uncovered during his excavations at Knossos, Evans tried to reconsider the dates attributed to the history of ancient Crete, finding corresponding data with the history of Troy, the Cycladic Islands and the rest of the Greek mainland, as well as with the history of Egypt and Mesopotamia, by comparing the Egyptian, Cretan and Syrophoenician objects which were discovered in this part of the world.

He suggested that the period which lay between the end of the n e o - l i t h i c   e r a and the invasion of the A c h a i o i be termed the M i n o a n Civilization, after King Minos.

Pondering more and more on the ceramic objects he was unearthing, Evans came to distinguish three separate epochs in the Minoan civilization : the E a r l y   M i n o a n   E p o c h (burnished, monochrome and painted vessels) ; the M i d d l e   M i n o a n (vessels in multicoloured designs on a dark-coloured ground ; these had been excavated at K a m a r e s and are termed 'Kamares Ware ;') and the L a t e   M i n o a n   e p o c h (vessels with dark-coloured designs on light-coloured ground).

This dating of Evans, with subsequent corrections, finally took the following form :-

| ERAS | CORRESPONDING EGYPTIAN DYNASTIES | DATES B.C. | CORRECTED FINAL DATES |
|---|---|---|---|
| Early Minoan | | | |
| First | 1st  –  3rd | 3400 – 2800 | A. 3200 – 2800 |
| Second | 4th  –  6th | 2800 – 2400 | B. 2800 – 2400 |
| Third | 7th  –  11th | 2400 – 2100 | C. 2400 – 1900 |
| | | | |
| Middle Minoan | | | |
| First | 11th – 12th | 2100 – 1900 | A. 1900 – 1800 |
| Second | 12th – 13th | 1900 – 1700 | B. 1800 – 1700 |
| Third | 14th – 17th | 1700 – 1550 | A. 1700 – 1600 |
| | | | B. 1600 – 1580 |
| | | | |
| Late Minoan | | | |
| First | 18th up to Tothmes | 1580 – 1450 | A. 1580 – 1500 |
| | | | B. 1500 – 1450 |
| Second | 18th up to Amenophes | 1450 – 1400 | 1450 – 1375 |
| Third | 18th – 20th | 1400 – 1200 | 1375 – 1100 |

But today the dates furnished by Evans have been revised further; Evans had worked from the changes in pottery styles revealed by the different strata. Today, the main periods of the life of the Minoan palaces are sometimes taken as a more simplified basis. This form of dating has been suggested by G l o t z, M a t z and N. P l a t o n; it is based mainly on the destructions suffered by the palaces. (1)

A. Pre-palatial Era
1st phase . . . . . . . . . . . . . . . . . 2600 – 2400 B.C.
2nd » . . . . . . . . . . . . . . . . 2400 – 2200 B.C.
3rd » . . . . . . . . . . . . . . . . 2200 – 2000 B.C.

B. Old or First Palatial Era
1st phase . . . . . . . . . . . . . . . . . 2000 – 1900 B.C.
2nd » . . . . . . . . . . . . . . . . 1900 – 1800 B.C.
3rd » . . . . . . . . . . . . . . . . 1800 – 1700 B.C.

C. Neo-palatial Era
1st phase . . . . . . . . . . . . . . . . 1700 – 1600 B.C.
2nd » . . . . . . . . . . . . . . . . 1600 – 1500 B.C.
3rd » . . . . . . . . . . . . . . . . 1500 – 1400 B.C.

D. Post-palatial Era
1st phase . . . . . . . . . . . . . . . . . 1400 – 1300 B.C.
2nd » . . . . . . . . . . . . . . . . 1300 – 1200 B.C.
3rd » . . . . . . . . . . . . . . . . 1200 – 1100 B.C.

# THE PERIOD OF THE FIRST AND SECOND PALACES

Knossos increased in prosperity from about 1900 B.C. when building started on the first palace; this was a stronghold temple, workshop and warehouse for storing goods and treasures all in one.

This period was one of exceptional trade expansion; the superiority of the island of Crete in the Aegean Sea was so great that the islands of Melos, Delos and Thera eventually counted but as vassals of the great island. A decisive factor assuring the transcendent prosperity of Crete was her trade with Egypt. She came to gain a firm place in the trade of ancient Egypt owing to her multicoloured vases and her ornaments.

But by about the year 1700 B.C. the palaces of Knossos were destroyed.

(1) Hutchinson : "Minoan Chronology" (Antiquity 1954).

Was it an invasion by Indo-Europeans ? But if so, who could be the people to muster a fleet strong enough to crush the naval hegemony of Crete? Or was it, perhaps, an attack made by the Egyptians ? Could it rather be due to a war between Malia, Knossos and Phaistos ? Or, was it due to a very strong earthquake ? This does seem to have been the most probable cause...

A new era of prosperity, however, starts once more for Crete without showing any breach or gap in her civilization. The island's wealth goes on progressing ; no alteration or change is detected in her art or in her local characteristics. The old palaces are rebuilt with architectural innovations, too, and more stately and more beautiful than before. It all involved a steady continuation of an upward trend.

A new period of prosperity and civilization is detected and it starts deploying in central and eastern Crete – a prosperity and a civilization quite peculiar and grandiose, one which came to embellish the Mediterranean Sea, one which was to be a forerunner of the Hellenic classical civilization.

Crete floats in such a splendour of light, in such exquisite climate, in such an exuberance of production from its soil that the Minoans could but be most optimistic in disposition and they must have shaken away at once the terror and despondency inflicted on them by the calamity which had struck

*The Goddess of the serpents (Museum)*

them. The amenities they so lavishly enjoyed wakened them at once to start creating once more, to search for beauty of forms and colours.

Exceptionally successful excavations have made it possible now to appraise the value of the amazing Minoan civilization and its characteristics and to fathom the breadth and the duration of its brilliancy ; it was indeed these factors which prepared and hastened the great feat of the Hellenic ci-

vilization which followed on the Greek mainland. Skilled workmen and artists of that epoch were able to revel in producing wonderful works by relying mainly on designs made, according to legend, by that gifted architect D a i-d a l o s.

But let us study closely these ruins of the wonderful works of the palace of Minos by wending our way through them and imagining their former grandeur.

The buildings have a rectangular form. This allows the subsequent addition of new halls, workshops and corridors. These buildings are known to have contained some o n e t h o u s a n d rooms, and these had antichambers, balconies, passages, staircases, shafts for the conveyance of light, etc. The whole of these works together marked out the palatial buildings as unique.

Wherever it was not possible to provide windows, they built in suitable shafts for carrying down the light. This indirect lighting and ventilation proves the prodigious progress of the Minoans in architecture at a time when Europe still knew primitive conditions. The entire set of buildings was supplied with a drainage system for leading off rain waters as well as a plumbing system made of clay pipes which conducted everywhere both drinking water and water used for washing. Moreover these pipes

*The Prince with the Lilies
(Wallpainting-Museum)*

had one end narrower than the other, thus imparting momentum and pressure to the water passing through them, and fitted perfectly, forming a wonderful conduit line.

The drinking water was obtained from a source which was on Mount 'Youchta' at a distance of about 10 kilometres. The water from the source was transported in earthen piping which went down and up the intervening ground slopes passing the currents which lay on the way on little and narrow bridges. Some sections of this aqueduct were found inside the palace in the eastern wing as well as on the southern slope of the hill.

As the source of the water was on a very high level, the water reached easily the hill Kefala on which the palace was built.

For the first time in the palace a real aqueduct was used.

Through all these devices, the skilled workmen succeeded in presenting one of the finest buildings ever known ; this was indeed an amazing piece of work, indicating a conception of the highest degree and an execution most precise and accurate in every detail. Indeed, what amazing grace must have been imparted by the many balconies, towering one above another as they were ! And even more so, the lines of vaults and the magnificent and stately entrances !

Bricks placed on wooden rafters supported by a line of central columns formed the roofs. Gypsum plaster or slabs lay on the bricks. The light shafts, the windows made of fine parchment soaked in some hardening oil, the plumbing and drainage system – all in place and perfect... it is thus that comfort was secured by the occupants – comfort almost unknown anywhere else at that remote time. GLOTZ, in his book "THE AEGEAN CIVILIZATION" writes : "Here are the abundant and original features which characterize the palace of Knossos : the easy communication between the numerous apartments, the relaxation and repose in the most modern sense of the words, the harmonious stateliness

*Crater decorated with plastic flowers of Kamaraic style 2000 - 1700 B. C. (Museum)*

of the details, the love of the spectacular and the picturesque surroundings, which love is revealed by the stately entrances as well as the superimposed turreted verandas and balconies, which allowed an easy view of the exquisite landscapes all-around."

If we wish to better understand the perfectness and the expediency of the architecture of the palace, we must let fly our imagination thousands of years back so as to catch a glimpse of those interminable halls with the Minoans going to and fro and the Minoan ladies in their luxurious Topless dresses strolling about the countless corridors or reposing in the flower – bedecked verandas of the palace, having their bosoms entirely bare without the least feeling of shame or even reserve. We sould try to fancy with eyes of imagination the priests and the priestesses going about their ceremonial

Μουσεῖον : Ὁ Πρίγκηψ. Βασιλεύς-Ἀρχιερεύς. Τοιχογραφία
             Ἀνάγλυφος ἐκ Κνωσοῦ.
Museum  : Relief-Fresco of the Priest. From Knossos
Musée   : Le Roi-prêtre. Fresque en relief de Knossos.
Museum  : Der Prinz Reliffresko aus Knossos.
Museo   : Il Principe Re-Sacerdote Capo - Affresco.

Κνωσός : Κλῖμαξ πρὸς ἄνω πατώματα.
Knossos : The stairs to the upper floors.
Knossos : L'escalier vers les hauts étages.
Knossos : Die Treppe zu den oberen Stockwerken
Cnòsso  : Scala che conduce ai piani superioni

Κνωσός : Δυτικαὶ Ἀποθῆκαι.
Knossos : West Magazines.
Knossos : Les Magazins occidentaux.
Knossos : Die Westmagazine.
Cnosso : Magazzini occideétali.

Κνωσὸς : Τὰ Νότια Προπύλαια
Knossos : South Propylaeum.
Knossos : Le Vestibule Sud.
Knossos : Südpropyläum.
Cnosso : I Propilei Sud

duties of worship of their Deities, or leading their ritual dances, or offering their sacrifices on the altars.

It is only in this way that we might form an idea about those people in that bygone epoch.

This period, which was named "the G o l d e n   A g e" of Crete reached its culmination about the year 1450 B.C.

It was about then that all the sites of the island suffered a major destruction. This may have been caused by attackers or, as professor Sp.

*Guards*

Marinatos maintains, it might have been due to a terrific eruption of the volcano on the island of Thera or Santorini. Some have argued that the island of Sandorini is to be identified with the legendary Atlantis; but if the stories in Plato have any historical basis, then Crete itself must have been Atlantis.

However this may be, all the sites were destroyed though Knossos recovered immediately, probably with the first arrival of Mycenaean settlers who adapted the written form of the Minoan language for their own language, Mycenaean Greek, which was used on the tablets from the Palace of Knossos. Then Knossos itself was destroyed as a palace around 1400 B.C. The marks of the conflagration are visible in the remains today. *

One of the reasons which led the Minoans to give great significance to an infernal deity must surely have been the terrific geological convulsions which they had known in their time. So they came to believe that the Forces of Nature were hiding in a subterranean world and that it was in that Underworld that preparations were constantly being made for the reappearance of the good produce of the earth on its surface from year to year. The symbol of the underground goddess was the s e r p e n t, who later came to be considered as beneficent and turned out finally as a domestic emblem. The figure of the Bull, too, is included among the underground symbols, as the force of the bull was connected with that of the earthquakes and was described as "he who shakes the earth."

* One of the building materials used in the palace was timber. Most of the columns were wooden and were made of thick trunks of cypresses; also made of wood were all those parts which are today painted in light grey colour. As to why timber had been preferred this must have been due to selection of antiseismic material.

The creation and formation of the Mycenaean civilization on the mainland of Greece may have been helped by people who fled from the earthquakes and destruction of Minoan Crete. Prior to the destruction many valuable Minoan works of art in silver and stone had gone to Mycenae and the Minoans had established actual settlements in the Aegean islands.

The establishment of the Minoan Cretans in the island of Kythira has been confirmed by the excavations of Professor H u x l e y and Mr. Coldstream there. So also did the excavations of Professor C a s k e y at A g h i a I r e n e of the island of K e a. Earlier work had revealed a Minoan settlement at Triada on Rhodes.

After the destruction of the Palace of Knossos about 1400 B.C life did not come to an end there. Homer included in his epics the participation of Knossos in the Trojan War through her king, Idomeneus and his friend, Meriones. Eighty ships were sent to the Greek forces.

## WRITING

The problem of the way the ancient Minoans put their words into writing is of capital importance for a fuller understanding of their civilization. There is no doubt that the Minoans knew how to write : inscribed lumps of clay used for sealing, tablets, bars and labels, all of clay, give ample witness of that. But the decipherment of their language has met with difficulties ; even today it has not been fully achieved.

*The disk of Phaistos*

Following the discovery of the tablets Evans distinguished more than one form of Cretan writing.

1. During the first and second Middle Minoan periods a hieroglyphic system, called Hieroglyphic «A», was developed. This has about 91 hieroglyphic signs.

2. During the second Middle Minoan period a second system came in with inscriptions on clay bars and small tablets and seals carved in hard stones. This system, Hieroglyphic «B», has about 95 signs of which about 51

are common to those of system «A». The signs of «B» are less clumsy and their forms more plastic.

3. Already in the second, and fully in the third.Middle Minoan period linear signs occur. This is Linear Script «A», the best known Minoan writing system.

4. In the second Late Minoan period a new linear script occurs at Knossos. This is Linear Script «B», probably based on «A» since they have many signs in common. But «B» also has new signs. Both systems are syllabic, that is they use groups of syllabic signs as words.

Apart from Knossos the Palace of Malia has produced much Hieroglyphic material, while Aghia Triada and the Palace of Zakro have been the main sites for Linear Script «A», Knossos for «B». On the Greek mainland hundreds of tablets were found in the Palace of Pylos by B l e g e n in 1939, and others have come from Mycenae and Thebes. The signs on them are in the same script as those of Linear Script «B» from Knossos.

Evans begun the interpretation of the Minoan signs. Other workers, in addition to Evans, used likenesses between a number of Minoan signs and Cypriot characters. Brozny, who worked on Hittite and other languages, did not confine himself to the Cypriot script but resorted also to Phoenician and Hittite and other scripts of the early periods. The Bulgarian philologist G e o r g i e v believes that the Cretan and the Mycenaean tablets were written in an Indo-European language similar to Greek.

But it was M I C H A E L  V E N T R I S, who had been a cryptographer in the British Royal Air Force, who used the methods of code-deciphering. These depend on the frequency and position of the signs as well as on the recognition of the vowels and the distinction of the gender. Proceeding in this manner he succeeded in discovering correcpondence between the signs of a four-syllable group and the word A m n i s o s (a place on the coast not far from Knossos and which is mentioned by Homer). Other examples revealed similarities between Minoan/Mycenaean signs and other Greek words. It became evident that the Knossos Linear Script «B» tablets were written in an archaic form of Greek. However there are many points which still remain obscure in the early Aegean scripts. The Linear «A» system has not yet been deciphered; what could it hold in store for us ? Even so one can well understand the consequences which the discovery of Ventris in collaboration with Chadwick (1) had generally on the history of ancient Greece. In the final period of the palace of Knossos a form of Greek is sopken.

(1) Ventris died in 1956. Chadwick explained the method of his collaborator in his book THE DECIPHERMENT OF LINEAR B. New York, 1960.

# RELIGION

The Minoan civilization was deeply religious. Not only did religion influence the art of the Minoans; it affected all their activities. One central deity seems sovereign in Minoan religion. The mother Goddess or the Goddess of the fecundity of the earth, who reigns over the animal and vegetable world. Sitting prettily on a root of the t r e e  o f  l i f e, she is accompanied by various animals : serpents, lions, birds. Near her appears also o n e male deity, who is at the same time both her son and her lover. This is the lover who imparts fecundity to the great deity – N a t u r e. He is the producer of life who symbolizes victory over death as well as regeneration in nature....

This male god has a force proportionate to that of the goddess mother. As she comes down from heaven, he also does, imparting on earth either fecundity or death. There are some important reasons which advocate the opinion that such a male deity was believed to exist. For example: certain symbols : the d o u b l e  a x e, the figure-of-eight  s h i e l d.

"The Cretan religion has rendered more lively the figurative representations" of her gods by devising symbols which outlined clear comparisons with them's (CHARLES PICARD).

*Bull's Head Rhyton*

The Minoans deified nature and adored her in the figure of the great goddess who appears in three different cycles: the c e l e s t i a l, the t e r r e s t i a l and the u n d e r g r o u n d.

The more impressive places of the religion of the Minoans were mostly the natural large caves : the I d a i o n  A n t r o n, the D i k t a i o n  C a v e, the C a v e r n  of  E i l e i t h y i a, and others. One can form a rather good idea of the religion of the Minoans by studying the offerings of the faithful, the sacred ceremonial vessels, the idols of the Deity and, more particularly, the liturgical representations in miniature figuring on vessels or carved on stone seals, much of which has been brought to light through the extensive excavations.

The Minoan World contains solid proof of a high civilization. That World succeeded in rising intellectually to a point of political unity and religious perfection and, as we have said already, such conditions constitute a good proof of great progress. Moreover, as religion is always a mirror of the spiritual and moral attainments of a people, through her Minoan civilization, Crete was more than any other country destined to end in the idea of monotheism.... as she did.

## LABYRINTH

It is difficult for anyone visiting the palace of Knossos for the first time to be able to find his way by himself alone. This was the case at all times and in every epoch. The belief, therefore, came to prevail that the p a l a c e of Knossos was a dreadful place where one gets lost and cannot find one's way out. It is in this way that the myth about the l a b y r i n t h was created. Labyrinth was also the name of the palace of Minos because the palace was dedicated to the sacred L a b r y s, the word labrys meaning a d o u b l e a x e. This is the second of the sacred symbols or emblems of the ancient Minoans of Crete.

The double axe plays, as a symbol, a remarkable role in the Minoan religion. During the Middle Minoan era we find it on columns, on vessels, on precious stones, etc. The axes so discovered include axes in gold, in silver, in copper and in stone.... One wonders : were they honouring with this emblem the instrument of the sacrifice ? But there are other accepted possibilities as well.

The gods of Asia, the lords of thunder, were armed with a double axe as a weapon. Much has also been discussed about the twin feature of the axe. Two-edged, as it was, it must have symbolized the presence of both the idea of a weapon as well as the union of the Deity with the God.

*The two sacred Minoan emblems : "the horns of the bull" and the double axe"*

On the other hand, it might also have been simply the emblem of Minos who, as we have mentioned, was considered the personification of God on Earth. "L a b r y s" was the word used by the Greeks to name the double axe. The word "l a b y r i n t h" comes from this word, and the palace of Minos was also known as "the palace of the double axes." (1)

The best words of praise for all the wonderful representations and the exquisite wall paintings were uttered by Evans who, upon discovering them during his excavations, said : "The parks of Knossos do indeed precede the parks of Versailles in France by some three thousand years and over.."

For indeed a thousand years later, the famous hanging gardens of Babylone were considered by the Greeks of the classical era as being one

(1) The etymology of the words l a b r y s - l a b y r i n t h is discussed by AZAVEDO ("SAGGIASUL LABIRINTO," Milan, 1953).

of the seven wonders of the world. And yet superior works and gardens did exist much before the wonder of the gardens of Babylon, namely the works and gardens of the palaces of Minos on Greek soil, in the island of Crete, the existence of which was not even suspected by the Greeks of the classical period long before the advent of Christ......

Some of the palatial buildings had two, othes three, or four and five storeys. All supported their facades on thick columns, thinner at the base

*Acrobatics on a Bull*

and thicker on top ; some columns were painted black, others white and others red. Majestic staircases led to the upper storeys and the roofs. As a decorative topping the columns had the sacred emblem of Crete – the horns of the bull – which was carved on stone and was painted in gold so that it shone brightly in the Cretan afternoon sun.

## MYTHOLOGY AND LEGENDS

The island of Crete was one of the beloved places and themes in Greek mythology. Central in her legends, between myth and history, comes the person of King Minos, son of Zeus and Europa, heavenly and earthly king, law-giver to Crete and judge in Hades. He was brother of Radamanthys, (who reigned over the Island of the Blessed) and of Sarpedon, husband of Pasifae (daughter of the Sun and Persyis) and father of Ariadne, Phaidra, Glaucos and Androgeos and, as well, lover also of Scylla, of Prokriti and of Vrytomartis.

The nature of the power of the king was religious : "Sovereign - Priest" says Evans. Minos was on Earth the personification of the male deity of fecundity who, in turn, was the master of the thunderbolt and the rain and was related to the Mother Goddess, who personified the Earth.

In reality the legend of Minos corresponds to a historical truth ; it symbolized the sea power of the Minoans who dominated once in the Aegean.

According to the legend, Minos called on Neptune (Poseidon), the god of the sea, to send him an animal for sacrifice so as to demonstrate his great sea power ; the animal so sispatched was a big and very beautiful bull ; so Minos wentand sacrificed in its place another ordinary bull of his, retaining the divine beautiful bull. Enraged by this act, Neptune went then and took revenge on Minos by inspiring his beautiful bull not only with an intoxicated fury but also a strong sexual urge of the bull for the person of P a s i f a e, the wife of Minos.... In accordance with the legend, copulation between the divine beautiful bull and Pasifae did take place through a ruse of Daidalos, who went and constructed from copper a cow in which Pasifae was enclosed : eventually the divine bull was able to have sexual intercourse with Pasifae through this ruse. The legend goes on to say that the offspring from this union was a freak monster by the name of A s t e r i o s or A s t e r i o n who, owing to his monstrous figure, was surnamed M i n o t a u r.

*Theseus*

In his turn, Minos went on and had Daidalos build an intricate labyrinth * in order to hide the monstrous offspring of Pasifae from public view. Later Theseus was able to kill the Minotaur with the help of Ariadne, daughter of Minos, who was charmed by the exceptional beauty and vigour of Theseus and came to love him.

*A r i a d n e*

According to Pausanias, Asterion was killed by Theseus. In fact Pausanias mentions that there existed on the Acropolis of Athens a relief representing Theseus wrestling with what was known as the bull (the 'tauros') of Minos, who was either a m a n o r a w i l d a n i m a l. This narrative

* The legend does not cancel the explanation given on page 19

23

went on even to create the belief that Pasifae had given birth to a son by having sexual intercourse with Daidalos himself and not with any bull, as Daidalos himself secretly was in love with Pasifae and, in order to satisfy his passion for her, he went and invented the whole ruse of the copper cow and the Minotaur in order to have Pasifae enclosed in the copper cow, where, without her knowing who was who or what was what, he finally had his way. The offspring was Asterion, who was surnamed Minotaur simply owing to the narrative of the copper cow and the bull. But while Pasifae might have been tricked, clever Minos was not in the least : he guessed the ruse of Daidalos and threw both Daidalos and his son Ikaros in prison. The known escape

*Daidalos and Pacifae*

from prison of both Daidalos and Ikaros provoked the wrath of Minos who, in revenge, pursued them as far as Sicily where he died, but... not before establishing there a new kingdom.

According to a third version of this legend, Minotaur was a son of a certain admiral of Minos who, owing to his robustness, was surnamed T a u r u s. (Plutarch relates that, with the help of Ariadne, Theseus wrestled with an admiral of King Minos, whom he knocked out). Greek Mythology seems, indeed to have been so extremely fertile in inventive imagination, that it managed to retain all the three versions of this legend. And the legend does not stop here in any of its versions: it goes on to relate that the

monster born was regularly devouring year-in- year-out inside the labyrinth of the palace of Minos the seven young girls and the seven young boys who were shipped over to King Minos every year from Athens as a 'tribute of blood' imposed by Minos on the Athenians in expiation for the murder of Androgeos his son.

But the truth about those seven young girls and the seven young boys who were sent over to Crete every year not only from Athens but also from other cities from the Greek mainland and the islands, may have been that they went over to Crete to take part with the Minoans in certain celebrations held yearly and known as the celebrations of "G o o d  H a r v e s t' in honour of the goddess mother – the goddess of the fecundity of the earth. These celebrations comprised also some bullfights or dangerous field ath-

letics done on the backs of bulls and their horns in special arenas provided for the purpose ; these athletic games were called 'taurokathapsia' and it was the said seven young men and the seven young girls  from abroad who, after taking a long and difficult training, performed various acrobatics on the backs of bulls. A peculiar wall painting, now preserved at the Museum of Heraklion, illustrates such an acrobatic performance :  a skilled athlete is shown making a dangerous leap on the back and around the horns of a not too co-operative bull ; while with extended arms and very strained muscles a young girl makes ready to receive and hold him.  A second young girl prepares to make her leap ans is seen suspended in the air and holding the horns of the bull as if she were practicing on parallel bars in a gymnasium. .

It can be guessed that many of these hardy youths met their death in this contest, whence the legend that the Minotaur devoured them in distant Crete.

*Types of Minoan Houses (Faience)*

However that may be, the games of 'taurokathapsia' were to the Minoans both a traditional and a cherished celebration. Was this celebration held only for recreation or was it held in honour of the deity which the bull symbolized ? Or was it held to commemorate an alleged victory of the Goddess-Mother who had subdued and tamed the animal ?

# MINOAN  WORLD

From the very first day the discovery was made that there was an ancient Minoan World preceding the Hellenic World, that Minoan World appears now for sure to have been very active and attractive from the utensils and articles dug up, for these articles are surprisingly or very high quality both for delicate technique of manufacture and the luxurious materials they are made of. One finds oneself tarrying for hours examining each and every one of them in admiration and astonishment.

So attractive is this World, too : replete, vigorous, rich, multiform and pleasant, creative of incomparable art, refined and subtle, full of grace and commanding a technique which seems to have composed hymns of praise to life and to the joy of life.

The Cretan artists succeeded in creating an order and a style which belongs exclusively to them ; its radiance expanded all over the Greek islands and to the mainland.

Today we are able to admire the Minoan era in the architectural master-pieces and on the exquisite wall paintings of the palace of Knossos. These present to us the whole charm and beauty of perfection through their lines and their pictures, their harmonious surfaces and sizes, the details of the plants, animals, shells, lotuses appearing in the paintings, not to mention the vi-rility of the men and women shown in acrobatics on the horns of bulls, of fighting bulls, and the femininity of very elegant women shown in poses of grace and coquetery.

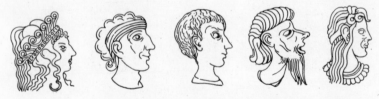

*Minoan Types*

The Royal mansions, too, were very lavishly supplied with wall paintings, in the subjects of which the artists had drawn inspiration from the animal and the vegetable world. The red and blue colours dominate, and through these colours the artists succeeded in creating a wonderful legendary world, something between reality and dream.

But it was not that the Royal mansions were the only abodes of such luxury. The houses of the people too, presented a special and astonishing comfort, as these also were provided with ample and spacious rooms, bathrooms, and bath tubs and pipes conducting water to the living quarters. The household vessels and kitchen utensils, such as the dishes, the cups and kraters, the flower vases etc. whether engraved or painted, so delightful in creative composition, impart an exquisite beauty.

On our latest 'Topless' fashion the Minoans of old have also certainly preceded us : their statues and frescoes show pictures of elegant women, beautifully dressed but topless as well...To one of these pictures depicting a

woman Evans gave the title 'the Woman from Paris.' When one conptem-
plates such Minoan pictures as 'La Parisienne' or 'the Goddess of the Serpents,' one cannot but feel that our present-day directors and initiators of
elegant fashions would turn pale before such advance elegance in Minoan
Crete.

The same feeling prevails when one contemplates other pictures of
Minoan women : rich bosom, waist slim, hips rounded, face outlines ir-
regular, eyes large and vivid, nose small and tilted up, lips full and crimson-
red, long hair falling gracefully on the shoulders with little locks of hair
ornamenting the forehead. Her dress,
made of elegant heavy cloth, wholly
covers the lower part of the body to
the ankles and has the form of a bell.

*Giant cask*          *Pitchèr (amphore)*          *Rhyton*

A double belt girdles the slim waist and the breasts, quite naked, pop out
from an elegant corset which closes on the back high up in a beautiful bow.
She wears a head-dress which has the form of a skull. The whole appearance
is so fascinating, alluring and extraordinarily attractive that it has been a
source of plenty of copies and imitations. Even in Egypt we can see now
on ancient Egyptian wall paintings graceful Egyptian women wearing Minoan fashions. It is quite possible, therefore, that the Minoan style was the
fashion in other places at that time exactly as the Parisian fashion is mostly so now in our days.

A prominent Greek archaeologist describes the Minoan civilization as follows: "The anguish of death was crushed nearly completely under the rejoicings which throbbed in every direction; the whole of life was animated by an ardent faith in the Goddess Nature – the spirit throughout the world of creation – the goddess who inspired harmony.

It was on such beliefs that the urge of the Minoans to create art, to have peaceful co-existance among themselves, to abhor tyranny, to respect the Law, was surely based. Personal ambition was quite unknown even among the leading classes. Thus, no name whatever of any Minoan has ever been connected with any creative work, nor has the name of any Ruler been extolled for any particular act of his. It is for this reason that the nature of the Minoan civilization is so different from those of the Egyptians and of the Orient, where quite contrary principles prevailed. The spiritual flexibility of the Minoans thrived and grew in their application to seafaring which spurred their imagination. Besides this, their Mediterranean temperament certainly helped them to develop an extraordinary energy and activity.

*La Parisienne*
*(Fresco in Museum)*

Archaeological evidences convince us that their private life reached in that by-gone age a large degree of refinement and comfort. Not only were the homes perfectly adapted to the practical needs of life, but their environment, too, was set to form an exquisite background. The close ties which the Minoans had with Nature inspired them to architectural arrangements which allowed them to enjoy freely their amenities, while at the same time they could easily adapt themselves to climatic alterations. Verdant gardens stretched around the houses and especially the palaces and in some places inside the houses as well; they used to keep flowers in a multitude of decorated vessels and this augmented still more the sensation of the presence of Nature everywhere. For relaxation and rest, the Minoans had especially provided arcades and galleries for sheltered walks, terraces, rest houses, even bathrooms with running water.... For the children there were special apartments provided in a number of places with small bathrooms. Their clothes, light garments for the men, variegated dresses – Topless, but accentuating the slenderness of the waist – for the women, did ensure for the body of both sexes that freedom of movement, vividness and suppleness which the world lacked so badly in the Middle ages and in Victorian times ! Sometimes the hair was left uncovered, with very skilful coiffures, or hats with narrow or broad rims were worn. Care for a good appearance held an important place in the life of the Minoans : they painted themselves, they applied shadows on their eyes, they thinned their eyebrows, they curled, frizzled and gave their hair colours of their liking,  and they applied plenty of perfumes to their bodies; what is more important, they adored athletics and gave plenty of exercise to their  bodies – a not unimportant  way  to good looks''...

Seated young Ladies

The three large palaces of Minoan Crete,  that of K n o s s o s ,  o f  P h a i s - t o s  and of M a l i a , as well  a  fourth  palace newly discovered by the archaeologist P l a t o n  i n K a t o  Z a k r o s ,  S i t i a , have given us a vivid picture of the  peculiar  civilization of that remote era of Crete, though no part of their fabulous treasures escaped plunder and sacrilege. Despite all, the meagre picture gained now by us is indeed amazingly rich in that it furnishes more than ample proof of the dazzling grandeur of those former times.

Up to the beginning of this century only a very faint echo reached us. from all this throbbing civilization of old in Crete. This echo, too, tallied with a legend recited above about Theseus.

But, otherwise, the Minoan civilization was entirely unknown to us. It was only about the year 1900 A.D. that the renowned archaeologist and explorer S i r  A r t h u r  E v a n s started systematic excavations at Knossos. He worked at them persistently for 30 whole years. And he was rewarded : the excavations uncovered the amazing Palace of Minos, the «Little Palace», the «Royal Villa», the «Aqueduct», the «Guest House» (what is known as Karavan-Serai),  the «Sacred Sepulchre of Minos», the  «House of the High Priest», and  other buildings.

Besides their technical perfection, the buildings uncovered were, in conception and in point of utility and usefulness to man, quite the opposite to the buildings of ancient Egypt and ancient Asia. It was the very first architecture in the world the sensible aim of which was simply to serve man.

Evans has described the Minoan civilization as the most evolved and the most advanced of all the ancient civilizations of the world.

Writting on the subject of the Minoan civilization, the English philosopher and historian Arnold Toynbee says : "Emerging spontaneously and directly from primitive, barbaric conditions, this Minoan civilization was the result of the answer of man to the challenge of the sea and to his effort to adapt himself to impose himself on her." So, it must not be forgotten that

*A golden ornament (Museum)*

our much extolled Western Civilization proves far from having been spontaneous, as it emanates from the ancient Greek civilization which, in its turn, was but a product of the Minoan and perhaps the Egyptian civilizations. Surely our Western Civilization is but a product of many influences.


## THE SEAPOWER OF MINOS

Knossos was not a walled city, nor did any other city in Crete have walls. This means that the State of Minos was powerful and did not fear enemy attacks. We do not find fortifications anywhere. For many centuries the land benefited from a continual state of peace and this must certainly be the reason why the Minoan civilization evolved in complete freedom of action and progress...... This truth is due initially, perhaps, to the privileged geographical position of the island of Crete. The island lies in the centre of Eastern Mediterranean – a very convenient place from which to sail to distant parts.

The natural resources of the island, the progress made by its craftsmen, the luxurious life of its people, all tended to force the Cretans to go abroad in search of more raw materials which they needed for their handicraft, craftsmen, goldsmiths, metalworkers, materials such as gold, silver, ivory, precious metals. Probably the increasing pressure wrought by the general progress of the people of the island as well as the love, perhaps, of the islanders for adventure – these, too, may have played a role in the development of trade and commerce in the island.

Anyhow, from very early times, trade transactions between town and town become the order of the day. Every town or settlement has its own market, and so starts in every locality a trend towards specialization in some particular kind of work: at G o u r n i a handmade articles; weapons and jewels at K n o s s o s; copper tools at P r a i s s o s.

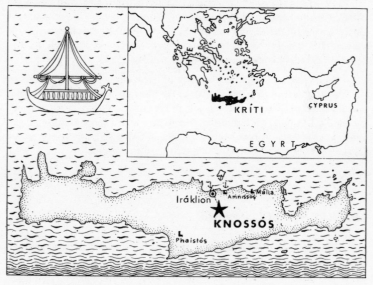

*The island of Crete, centre of Eastern Mediterranean.*

From the earliest Minoan eras, Cretan ships go riding on the seas. Whole forests of cypress and cedar trees abundantly supplied the necessary timber for building ships. The Cretan ship had a length of about 30 metres; her bow was richly bedecked and stood higher than the stern; she had comfortable banks for the rowers and carried two or three masts. Here was the Cretan vessel: light and always slender and refined and very proud and austere in her build.

The treasures which have been excavated, such as vases and frescoes, testify clearly through the representations of sea-urchins, octopuses, flying

31

fishes, dolphins and other sea animals, how progressive, rich and highly developed were the Minoans and how much akin and close to the sea and masters of distant navigation they had succeeded in becoming.

Thucydides, Herodotus and Plato advise us that the first masters of the sea were the Minoans and that the first King who built a navy was Minos.

It appears that King Minos secured through his great seapower considerable income... An ancient painting has saved for us the representation of a procession of tithepayers coming to pay homage to the Ruler of Knossos. In exchange King Minos watched over matters of peace and security, having rid the Aegean and adjacent areas from any attacks by would-be pirates. The seas were so to speak under police protection through the presence of a very mighty fleet manned by trained crews.

On a stretch of coast in the north of Crete along some ten kilometres we find three harbour installations which the Minoans used for their merchant marine and navy. These are : A g h i o i  T h e o d o r i (the present name of the locality), A m n i s o s and the river K a i r a t o s (present Katsambas), which is purported to have been navigable, allowing ships to sail up to the Palace of Minos where they could offload their cargoes.

## MOTHER OF ALL... PEACE

That the island enjoyed good administration, as well as wise and just legislation and laws, which brought along peace and prosperity, is vouched by the peaceful duration through long centuries of the Minoan civilization.

Agriculture, cattle-raising, fishing and especially hunting - were all regular pursuits of the Minoans. They cultivated the vine and the olive tree. Their art in weaving, their industry in ceramics and their pursuits in metallurgy, goldsmith's work and sculpture were quite advanced.

According to D i o d o r o s and A r i s t o t l e the Minoans stored provisions and other necessaries in large warehouses and, in years of bad harvests, these were distributed to the citizens in rations.

Evans maintains that this civilization continued for over o n e  t h o u-s a n d  y e a r s. It reached its pinnacle between the years 1700 and 1400 B.C. This period was named "the G o l d e n  E r a  o f  C r e t e."

Κνωσός : Βορεία Εἴσοδος.
Knossos : North Eutrance.
Knossos : L' etrée Nord.
Knossos : Nord - Eingang
Cnosso  : Entrata settentrionale

Κνωσός : Μέγαρον Βασιλίσσης.
Knossos : Queen's Megaron
Knossos : Megaron de laeine.
Knossos : Megaron der Köningin.
Cnosso : Megaron della Regina.

Κνωσός : Ὁ θρόνος τοῦ Μίνωος.
Knossos : The Throne of Minos.
Knossos : Le Thrône de Minos.
Knossos : Der Thron von Minos.
Cnosso : Il Trone di Minosse.

Κνωσός : Μέγα κλιμακοστάσιον : Ἡ αἴθουσα τῶν κιόνων.
Knossos : Big. Staircase : The saloon of the pillars.
Knossos : Le grand éscalier : La salle des colonnes.
Knossos : Grosse Treppe : Der Saal der Säulen.
Cnosso : Grande Scalinata : La sala delle clone.

The form of government of Crete was the absolute Monarchy. The King was the Supreme Ruler and the High Priest, all in one. But the regime which the King imposed must have been both very wise and meticulously just for, otherwise, it would not have been at all possible that the civilization of the island could have been preserved quite unbroken for such a length of time, nor that such a large population could have been sustained in continuous peace and prosperity.

# PLAN OF THE PALACE OF MINOS AT KNOSSOS

A. Western Entrance
B. Southern Entrance
C. Eastern Entrance
D. Northern Entrance
1 Central court

## A WESTERN WING

1. Central Court
2. West Court
3. Altars
4. Sacred Depositories
5. West Porch
6. West Magazines
7. Corridor of the Procession
8. Corridor
9. Prince
10. South House
11. Stepped Portico
12. South Propylaeum
13. Staircase Propylaeum
14. Columnar Shrine
15. Anteroom of the Pillar Crypts
16. Pillar Crypts
17. Vat Room
18. Temple of Repositories
19. Tall Pithos

### I LIVING ESTABLISHMENT

20. Anteroom
21. Throne Room
22. Inner Shrine
23. Staircase
24. Piano Nobile
25. Prisons of Minos
26. North Lustral Basin
27. NW Portico
28. Theatre
29. Grand Staircase
30. Hall of the Double Axes
31. King's Megaron
32. Queen's Megaron
33. Bath Room
34. Toilet Room
35. Treasury
36. Shrine of the Double Axes
37. E. Lustral Basin

## B EASTERN WING

### II INDUSTRIAL ESTABLISHMENT

38. Court of the Distaff
39. Toilets
40. House of the Sacred Tribune
41. S.E. House
42. Lapidary's Workshop
43. Potters' Workshop
44. Giant Pithoi
45. E. entrance
46. Corridor of the Draught Board
47. Water System
48. Medallion Pithoi
49. Corridor of the Bays
50. N.E. House
51. N.E. Magazines
52. Workshops
53. Magazines for Ceramics
54. Custom House
55. N. Entrance Passage

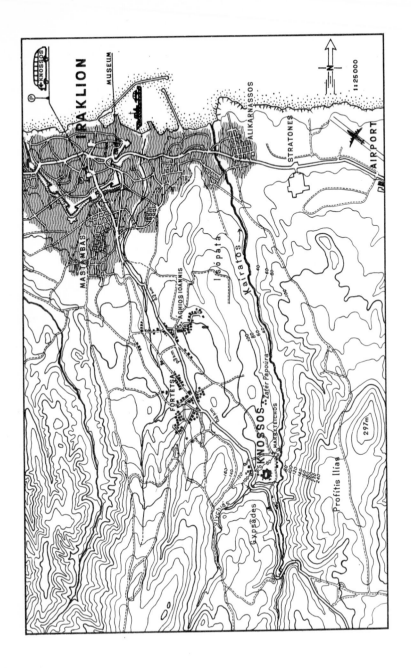

*A Minoan Procession in the island of Crete*

# VISIT TO THE PALACE OF KNOSSOS

Distance from Heraklion: 5 kilometres

Bus starting point: to Knossos, every 20 minutes from the harbour of Heraklion with intermediary stops at the Morosini Fountain and the Cornarou square.

Open to visitors: 7 a.m. to sunset.

## 1. AREA AND CHARACTERISTICS OF THE PALACE
(See map)

The shortest time required to visit the palace is one and a half to two hours.

The palace has four entrances, one from each point of the compass. Each entrance serves a particular purpose.

In size the palace occupies some 20.000 sq. metres and consists of two wings which have many floors; these wings lie to the west and to the east of a central large rectangular courtyard, (No. **1**), which occupies an area of 1.450 sq. m. This courtyard was, in its time, paved; it constitutes the focusing centre of the palace; at the same time it is the starting point for visiting the whole establishment and the surest way for visitors to find their orientations towards all its parts.

The courtyard generally constitutes a fundamental common feature of Minoan architecture ; in fact we find such courtyards in all Minoan palaces. They were used for lighting and ventilation, as well as for securing easy communications with the other wings of the palace, and perhaps also for holding religious liturgies in the presence of big crowds of Minoans.

## A. WESTERN ENTRANCE

(It is from here that we enter the palace today).

The Western Entrance, leading from the interior of the city of Knossos, was reserved for foreign persons of high rank. It is situated on the SW of

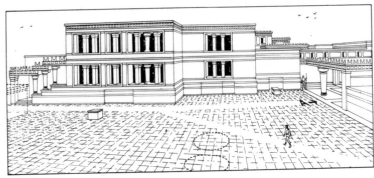

*Western Entrance. Western Courtyard.*

the large western courtyard just outside of the palace and consists of an arcade having one column, a g u a r d - h o u s e , a waiting room or aide-decamp-quarters (these contain frescoes representing acrobatics performed on the horns and backs of bulls), as well as a large passage which is bedecked with frescoes representing a procession of young men and women carrying or offering to the Goddess presents and votives.

## B. SOUTHERN ENTRANCE

The Southern Entrance is reached by a large paved road from the M e s a r a ; this road has a bridge over the torrent V l y c h i a which runs in the southern ravine of the K e f a l a hill. The entrance is an e s c a l a t-

ıng thoroughfare which, towards the top, ends in a short passage where a magnificent staircase led on to the central courtyard. At the end of the eastern part of the short passage there is a small vault and, under this vault, there is an underground cupola which is hewed in the rock ; most probably that was a secret entrance to the huge mysterious palace

*Southern Entrance*

Here was also the terminus of the road thoroughfare which traversed the island from the south. In its time it was thronged with caravans bringing goods from Egypt as well as the products from the rich plain of Mesara.


## C. EASTERN ENTRANCE

This entrance, which was reached by a downhill road, was provided with ramparts communicating with the inside through staircases leading to guardhouses. An open conduit for rainwaters, cut in the stone, was nearby. Evans believed that here were the palace laundries. From this entrance one could go to the Kairatos river and to the arena where the bullfights took place.

## D. NORTHERN ENTRANCE

This was the H a r b o u r  G a t e or the S e a  G a t e. Just before it there is the t e l o n e i o n  (customshouse), which was a wide gallery with thick square pillars. Following it there is a narrow uphill passage leading to the central c o u r t y- a r d. On both sides of this passage stand high walls carved with figures of t r i d e n t s,  a n d d o u b l e  a x e s.

On these walls there was a w a t c h - t o w e r the floor of which was on the same level as the central courtyard.

The w e s t e r n  w a- t c h - t o w e r, which is on the right of the person going up the entrance,

*The Northern Entrance*

has been erected as it was and is ornamented with a figure of a raging bull carved in relief and in bright colours.

## A  WEST  WING

This official wing of the palace — the religious — political wing — comprises :

a) "West Court" (No. **2**). This is a large, paved courtyard where the inhabitants of Knossos gathered on official celebrations. This court was traversed by little alleys slightly raised (the pompikoi dromiskoi — processional alleys).

It is presumed that during the celebrations the holy processions passed along them and that it was along them that the high ranking officials were carried on portable chairs.

In the west court there are also two "Altars" (No. **3**), the foundations of which are preserved, as well as the "Sacred Depositories" (No. **4**), which were cistern-like built-up holes where the refuse of the palace was dumped. As many pieces of broken vases were also found in them, they probably served as a spot where the vases were thrown after being emptied of their offerings, whence they also received the name "sacred depositories".

b)   "West Porch" (No. **5**). This was a roofed open space facing the court and had one pillar. To the south of the Porch there is a little Porter's Lodge which surely must have served for cheking the entrances.

c)   "West Magazines" (No. **6**). These are on the ground floor and consist of a group of eighteen oblong apartments having an entrance from a very long dark passage. Victuals were stored in the magazines as well as liquids of the State supplies in jars, some of which are preserved in the same spot today. These jars were estimated to have been around one hundred and fifty. In these magazines also the «treasures» (gold and other valuable objects) were kept in square boxes cut in their floor and in the floor of the passage. These boxes had an inner coating and were covered by stone slabs. But it is not excluded that they were also used for storing liquids, oil, etc.

On this spot of the palace hundreds of clay tablets were discovered, bearing written lists of the goods stored. These have been considered as one of the more important discoveries of the palace.

d)   «Corridor of the Procession» (No. **7**). Grandiose and imposing, this bore exquisite frescoes and has a line of columns. It started from the west court and leads towards the South. Then it turns to the left, following all the southern flank of the palace, and finally it turns again to the left to enter the Central Court through a "Corridor" (No. **8**) at the spot where today stands the "Prince" (No. **9**), or the Priest-King. This is a replica of the original which is exhibited in the museum.

Four hundred or more figures have been estimated on the designs which formed these famous frescoes of the procession. All of them show girls and young men carrying offerings to the deity.

e)   "South House" (No. **10**). This lies on a lower level at the South-Western corner of the palace. Most probably it served as residence of the nobles of the royal court, or of the aides-de-camp, or of some higher dignitary.

At the western flank of the South House ended the "Stepped Portico" (No. **11**) which led to the palace from its southern entrance for those who came from the interior of the island, after having previously passed from the

"Guest House" and through the road bridge of the torrent "Vlychia". This road bridge is still preserved in relatively good condition.

f) After the corridor of the procession we meet the grandiose South Propylaeum" (No. **12**). In this area horns of bulls were placed in large size. They are largely reconstituted and completed by a contemporary artisan. According to Evans they were placed on the top of the roof of the southern facade of the palace.

g) The person entering the palace from its western or southern entrance

*Magazines*

ends at the South Propylaeum and from there he is conducted to the upper floor of the west wing of the palace.

The South Propylaeum consists of two parallel walls between which there were two stands which formed a large opening occupied by a grand "Staircase" (No. **13**), the larger part of which has been reconstructed. In front of the opening there were two pillars which, together with the stands, supported the beams of the roof. Evans has re-erected the western flank of the Propylaeum.

Their adornment comprised many figures of cupbearers, of these only one is preserved, the famous "Cupbearer", an ideal specimen of Minoan manly beauty. A copy of the original lies here, the original itself being exhibited in the museum.

h)     The "Colymnar Shrine" (No. **14**). This comprises the "Ante-room of the Pillar Crypts" (No. **15**), the "Pillar Crypts" (No. **16**) ; in its centre stand square pillars (sacred pillars) made of gypsum with many engraved representations of the double axe the "Labrys" ; from this sacred symbol, according to one interpretation, as we have already said, the Minoan word 'Labyrinth' was derived, which means the shrine or the "Palace of the Double Axes" where the 'Labrys' was adored ; around the pillars on the floor there are channels and cavities which were used for channeling out the blood of the sacrifices or the liquids falling out from the libations ; the "Vat Room" (No. **17**), the "Temple of Depositories" (No. **18**), or the "Shrine of the Goddess," in which are preserved two basements crypts, in which were found

*Hall of the Throne*

the liturgical vessels made of clay; the "two Goddesses of the Snakes" (mother and daughter are at present exhibited in the museum) ; the "Cross ;" the "Sacral Knot," etc., and the "Tall Pithos," (No. **19**).

i)     Hall of the Throne : this consists of an "Ante-Room" (No. **20**), where those waiting sat on   built-up benches alongside the walls. In the middle of the hall there was a stone basin, containing water, for washing the hands- symbolic purification of the whole body.  It still  remains in the same spot. From the main Hall we enter the "Throne Room" (No. **21**), with built-up benches where the counsellors and the priests sat.

On the northern wall we face the superb throne of King Minos made of gypsum and still at the very spot where the Sea Lord Minos sat when he executed his duties as king. This is the oldest known throne in the world.

In accordance with a hypothesis of Evans, the Cretan Kings were at the same time also priests of the Great Goddess.

On the wall, just above and on each side of the throne, there is a fresco representing griffins, that is imaginary birds or animals, having the head of the eagle and the body of the lion, symbolizing the two powers of the king. The eagle, being the strongest bird, symbolized the executive authority of the priest and the lion, being the strongest animal on earth, symbolized the power of the king. The griffins symbolize also the triple deity ; the head the celestial, the body the earthly, and the tail the infernal deity. On the left side of the room there is a "Holy Basin", hewn in the floor. King Minos went down to this basin as the representative of the Goddess Mother Earth for religious meditation and prayer. Further up the room there was a shrine with a built-up table of offerings ("Inner Shrine") (No. **22**).

According to Evans there in the interior of the shrine the Priest King retired for fasting and for praying. This space was wholly dark and was lit by a stone lamp.

j)    Alongside the Throne Room there is a "Staircase" (No, **23**), which has 12 steps, most of which have been rebuilt. This staircase leads from the central Court to the upper floor of the West Wing – the "official" one. "PIANO NOBILE" (No. **24**). This has the shape of a porch with a high pillar at its centre and another one on its highest level. Both served supporting the roof.

Higher up than the level of the first floor the staircase forms a square which is served with two doors. Further west starts another staircase which is narrower and which leads to the second floor. The greater of this section has been re-constituted.

k)    Further north are the "Prisons of Minos" (No. **25**), built-up cistern-like dug-outs having a depth of 7-8 metres, where possibly those sent to prison were locked in. However, they may also have served as water tanks.

l)    North of the prison, to the left of the northern entrance of the palace and in front of the area of the theatre lies the "N o r t h e r n   L u s t r a l   B a s i n" (No. **26**), which has been wholly restored. It has a stepped descent, which was used by those who adored the Goddess Mother Earth for prayer, meditation and spiritual purification. Inside the basin many small pots were found which evidently contained liquids for washing.

Around the basin an area was formed which Evans named "Initiation Area".

44

To go into the basin one had first to be initiated, and then one entered the palace.

m)    To the east of the basin lies the "N.W. Portico" (No. **27**), which is a room with a line of doors and two pillars.

n)    To the N.W. of the basin lies the "Theatre" (No. **28**). This is a paved space in the form of an amphitheatre. From the East and the West it is framed by two wings which have many steps disposed as an amphitheatre. At the Eastern end of the Southern wing lies the "Royal Balcony" or the "Royal Box", from which King Minos ,with his suit, watched the holy dances and the other sporting events which evidently were of a religious nature. From the theatre the ancient "Sacred Road" starts leading to the "Little Palace". This is preserved marvellously and is paved with stone slabs. It seems that, following the sacred dances which were performed there, the Kings and the dignitaries were conducted in procession to the little palace, or they would start from the little palace and, in procession would reach the theatre where the kings welcomed the arrival of the goddess..

This theatre is probably the first stone theatre in the world.


## B    EAST WING

This was an establishment with several storeys used as a residence by the royal family ; its northern section housed the handicraft and industrial activities of the palace. It consisted of some very extensive buildings of perhaps five storeys each. These buildings stood on the various levels of the cutting east of the central court; this section was cut out of the side of the hill. A grand staircase, going down from the central court two storeys and to the ground floor, was provided with balustrades and pillars: it ascended at least two more storeys. As a magnificent building achievement this staircase is unique. It is, perhaps, the most imposing and the finest section of the palace of Minos and fortunately it has been preserved for us in very good shape.

The two storeys which have been partly reconstituted are similar and are connected to one another with smaller staircases. Lightshafts were provided for all inner apartments which, otherwise would have remained dark.

This east wing of the palace was devided into two parts : the southern which was lived in, and the northern which was the industrial area.

## I. THE RESIDENTIAL QUARTER

The southern section of the eastern wing, which comprises many apartments, is of special importance because it included the apartments of the kings as well as the halls used for presentations and receptions of important persons of that era and for audiences. It comprises :

a) The "Grand Staircase" (No. **29**). As we have said above this is one of the masterpieces of Minoan Architecture. It is composed of four flights of which the upper two have been restored, while the lower two are preserved as they were. The staircase received light from a large shaft, which lies in the eastern flank and is surrounded by a series of pillars.

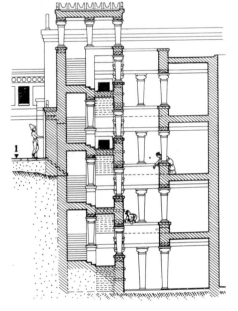

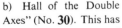
*The Grand Staircase*

b) Hall of the Double Axes" (No. **30**). This has an ante-room and a multi-columnar veranda lying eastwards and in the direction of the river Kairatos.

This section of the palace called the "King's Megaron" (No. **31**) and the hall has received its name from the frequent presence of double axes – a symbol carved on its walls. In this large hall, which is abundantly lit both directly from the court and through lightshafts, lie the remnants of a throne. Large figure-of eight shields were placed on the northern wall of the hall.

c)    Continuing, we enter the Queen's Megaron' (No. **32**). This comprises the private quarters of the queen which have rich ornamentations of frescoes. The fresco of the "Dolphins" crowns the door of the entrance and depicts also other fishes and crustaceous animals.

46

The "Bath Room" (No. **33**) ; the "Toilet Room" (No. **34**). (In this section of the palace and under a narrow staircase, a superb acrobat or leaper was discovered ; it is made of ivory ; today it is exhibited in the museum).

The "Treasury" (No. **35**). The "Shrine of the Double Axes "No. **36**); The "Lustral Basin" (No. **37**) ; The "Court of the Distaff" (No. **38**) (from the symbol of the distaff) ; here the ladies of the court gathered, spinning and weaving ; this court received light from a lightshaft : The "Toilets" (No. **39**) ; these were distinguished by their careful "modern" planning.

d)    In the interior of these quarters one can see the opening of a drainage system for the closets. This highly technical system in this section of the palace is better appreciated at the corner at the starting point of the dark pas-

*Hall of the Double Axes*

sage. The system is in elliptical form in the direction to the east of the Queen's Megaron and ends at some outflow towards the river Kairatos. In between lie smaller conduits, channels and little cisterns for the necessary control of the system. At the south eastern corner there is a "shrine" of the post-palatial period, with the "idols" of the "Great Goddess" with the "Dove" the sacred "Horns" and the "Double Cross". These are also tables for offerings.

e)    To the S.E. of this section of the palace there are also two houses, the "House of the Sacred Tribune" (No. **40**) and House called "South Eastern House (No. **41**).

## II. INDUSTRIAL QUARTERS

This section of the north eastern wing of the palace comprises various workshops and magazines.

a)    Lapidary's  Workshop  (No. **42**). Here is a store of blocks of porphyry imported from the Peloponnese. Above this room magnificent alabaster vases were made.

b)    «Potter's Workshop» (No. **43**). This room contains work benches and cavities for working the clay.

It is in this section of the palace that the superb fresco of the bull-fight, the "Tauromachia", was found ; today this is exhibited in the museum.

c)    "Magazines of the "Giant Pithoi" (No. **44**). These are ornamented with thick ropes in relief.

d)    The staircase which lies near-by leads to the east entrance (No. **45**) in the direction of the river Kairatos and the Arena of the bull-fights. To the west lies the "Corridor of the Draught Board" (No. **46**). In this corridor there was a magnificent royal gaming table of gold, ivory, rock crystal and lapis lazuli. This is why it has received the name ''Corridor of the Draught Board."

e)    At this point of the palace there is a grating below which one can see the pipes of the «Water System» (No. **47**). The shape of the pipes is narrower towards the top end and this shape was given to them so as to secure a continual pressure, the speed of the water inside the pipes thus overcoming every obstacle.

This system of water supply shows the high plumbing knowledge which the Minoans had mastered at that remote era.

West of this spot lies the "Magazine of the Medallion Pithoi "(No. **48**) as well as the "Corridor of the Bays" (No. **49**).

f)    Further north lies the "NE House" (No. **50**) and the "NE Magazines" (No. **51**).

g)    To the East of these Magazines there are some "Workshops" (No. **52**) as well as the "Magazines for Ceramics" (No.**53**), where many "Kamares" vessels were found. "Custom House" (No. **54**), N. Entrance Passage (No. **55**).

Some other monuments discovered outside the palace of Minos are :

**On the West of the Palace :**

**2.**   THE HOUSE OF THE FRESCOES

Just a little beyond the theatre there is a house with many rooms where

Μουσεῖον : Ἡ Παριζιάνα, Τοιχογραφία.
Museum  : The Parisienn, Fresco.
Musée   : La Parisienne, Fresque.
Museum  : Die Pariserin, Fresco.
Museo   : La Parigiana, Affresco.

Μουσεῖον : Οἱ Ρυτοφόροι, Τοιχογραφία.
Museum  : Rhytophores, Fresco.
Musée   : Rhytophores, Fresque
Museum  : Rhytophoroi, Fresko
Museo   : Portatori di ritoni, Affresco.

Κνωσός : Ὁ Ὑψηλὸς Πίθος.
Knossos : The Tall Pithos.
Knossos : Le Hout Pithos.
Knossos : Der Hohe Pithos.
Cnosso : Il Pitho gigante.

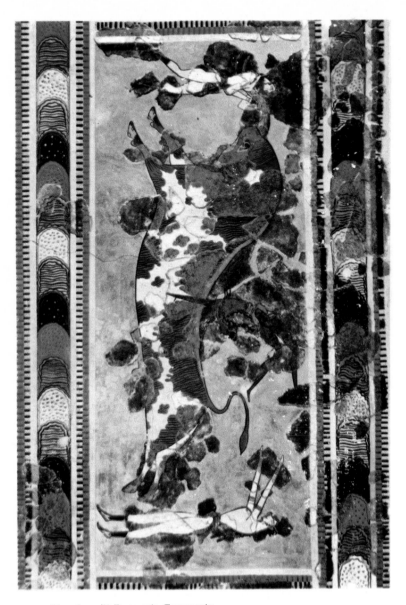

Μουσεῖον : Ἡ Ταυρομαχία, Τοιχογραφία.
Museum  : Toreador, Fresco.
Musée   : Combat de taureau, Fresque.
Museum  : Der Stierkampf, Fresko.
Museo   : Tauromachia, Affresco

exquisite frescoes were found ; the representations are of the vegetable and the animal kingdoms. Nearby there is a fine paved road which starts from the theatre and ends at the Little Palace.

### 3. THE LITTLE PALACE

The "Little Palace" lies at a distance of 130 metres to the north-west of the main palace and above the present-day car road. This is a Late Minoan assembly of buildings, the more important of which are : "the Gallery of the Peristyle," the big Mansion and the Sacred Pool, This Pool was converted during the third Late Minoan era to a Sanctuary, on the sacred bench of which were found some natural unworked stones belonging to some later religion of a fetish nature. Here also was found the superb libation-vessel made of serpentine in the form of a bull's head.

### To the East of the Palace :

### 4. THE ROYAL VILLA

This edifice is a real masterpiece and lies some 110 metres north-east of the big Palace ; it consists of a two-storey building, lit by a lightshaft. In one of the ground floor rooms of the mansion there is à throne and just in front of the throne a large lamp made of purple stone. To the north of this room there is a sacred crypt provided with a square pillar.

On the same floor the visitor can see grooves and cavities which served for the collection of the blood of the sacrificed animals or other liquids pertaining to the libations. The upper floor is arranged nearly like the balcony, where probably King Minos sat to watch the taurokathapsia games, of which mention has already been made, held on the grounds just below.

### 5. THE ARENA

As mentioned above, just a few yards below the Royal Villa, wide level ground stretches from a cavern lying on the hill slopes to the river Kairatos ; these grounds may have served as the arena for the bullfights, the celebrated t a u r o k a t h a p s i a  g a m e s, which were so dangerous to the Minoans, though so dearly attractive as well.

### To the South of the Palace :

### 6. THE GUEST–HOUSE (CARAVANSERAI)

This lies at about 200 metres to the south of the Great Palace. It is a roofed structure, the walls of which are decorated with coloured representations of partridges and other birds ; it has bathrooms supplied with water, bedrooms and a room known as the r o o m  of t h e  s p r i n g, from which water continues to flow even today. Deep inside this room there is a niche, where a lamp was placed, and the niche has projections on either side for votive offerings. Outside the Guest-house there is a stone basin for washing the feet and a little beyond stone trough with drinking water for animals.

### 7. THE HOUSE OF THE HIGH PRIEST

This lies to the South of the Guest-House and at a short distance from it under the modern car road and a little to the left of it. It was a Sanctuary ; at its entrance there is a box for offerings and, deep inside, a stone a l t a r between two columns ; it also contains some platforms for double axes.

### 8. THE ROYAL TEMPLE TOMB

This lies at about 450 metres to the South of the Great Palace and near the house of the High Priest, above the carroad. It consists of two floors ; the lower one, which is under ground, has a paved c o u r t - y a r d, an a r-c a d e (with two huge pillars bearing carvings of tridents), a r o a d paved with large slabs of gypsum and a c r y p t with two pillars. Deep inside the crypt there is a small room with a pillar in the middle ; the roof of this room is painted blue.

The visitor can see a small "cavity" at the north-east corner of this room; scattered in this cavity were found the skull and bones of a male; these may have been the skull and bones of the last Minos of Knossos. The upper floor was probably used as a sacred peristyle over the grave ; it has two pillars between which sacred horns in stone are erected.

## 9. THE MINOAN CEMETERIES

First there is the cemetery on the P r o p h e t e s  E l i a s  hill, oppo-site the Palace of Minos to the east. It is dated to the Middle and Late Mi-noan periods (1700-1200 B.C.). The tombs are cut as caves in the soft lime-stone rock.

Secondly there are the cemeteries of Z a p h e r  P a p o u r a  a n d I s o p a ta  to the north of the Palace. Both of these belong to the Late Minoan period (1450-1200 B.C.).

Finally there are the tombs on the Gypsadhes hill south of the Palace, These also for the most part belong to the third Late Minoan period.

When one takes into account the expanse of these cemeteries as well as the area covered by the Minoan buildings, it is calculated that the popula-tion of the Minoan city of Knossos may have been around 100.000.

## 10. ROMAN AND BYZANTINE ANTIQUITIES

Among the best preserved ruins from Roman times are :

1. T h e  V i l l a  o f  D i o n i s o s, to the North and near the V i l l a A r i a d n e  of Evans. Its floor is ornamented with an exquisite represen-tation in mosaics of Dionisos and his troupe of actors.

2. T h e  B y z a n t i n e  B a s i l i c a  C h u r c h  near the Villa.

3. T h e  M a c r o t i c h o n ; these are remnants of the wall of the city of Knossos from Roman times and they lie near the settlement which now bears the same name, North East of the Palace.

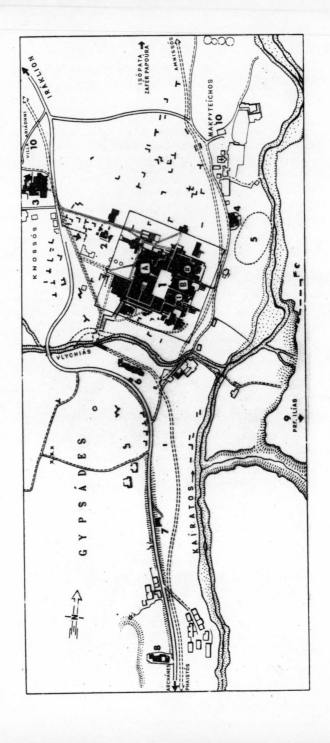

*Museum of Heraklion*

# ARCHAEOLOGICAL MUSEUM OF HERAKLION

The Archaeological Museum of Heraklion is in the eastern sector of the town of Heraklion and on the northern side of the Eleftheria square.

As a building it is one of the finest museum buildings in Greece.

The museum was founded by the Cretan savants Joseph Hadzidakis and Stephen Xanthoudidis and houses all the valuable collection of treasures of the ancient Cretan civilization in all of its manifestations.

Preserved in the museum are the antiquities excavated at K n o s s o s, Phaistos, Malia, Gortys, Aghia Triada, Mochlos, Gournia, Zakros and in the various caves, K a m a r e s, I d a i o n Antron, Dictaion Antron, Arkalohorion, Eileithyia etc.

By sheer coincidence these excavations started at the time the Island's status of autonomy was proclaimed. This was an exceptionally happy coincidence because all the antiquities excavated have remained in the island.

It is exactly for this reason that the museum of Heraklion is unique and is known all over the world.

Apart from one room set aside axclusively for scientific study and research, the museum comprises twenty more halls containing the exhibits ; these are arranged in chronological order with the following groups of finds : neolithic, prepalatial, cemeteries, mansions from central Crete, Geometrical and Greek graves, sarcophagae, frescoes.

Among the museum halls there is also the Y a m a l a k i Collection

containing the rare Minoan seals made of stone, a golden crown, golden cup and a bronze r a m - b e a r e r. The arrangements in this hall have particularly been taken care of by the distinguished archaeologist and Curator of Antiquities in Crete, Dr. Stylianos Alexiou.


## VISIT TO THE MUSEUM OF HERAKLION

The museum is open to visitors from 08.00 to 13.00 and from 15.00 to 17.00 daily, except Monday afternoons when it remains closed. On Sundays it is open from 10.00 to 13.00.

A minimum of one or two hours is necessary for the visit.

To assist the visitors we mention here the most important objects exhibited in the show-cases. The halls are numbered in Latin numbers.


### Ground Floor

#### HALL I

| | |
|---|---|
| 6000 - 2000 B.C. | Finds of the neolithic and pre-palatial Minoan civilization. |
| Show-case No. 7 : | Masterpieces of vessels in stone found in tombs excavated in the little island of M o c h l o s off the north eastern coast of Crete. |

#### HALL II

| | |
|---|---|
| 2000 - 1700 B.C. | Finds of Minoan civilization of the era of the ancient Minoan palace, excavated from the palaces of Knossos and Malia. |
| Show-case No. 23 : | Famous vessels of Kamares form, the thickness of the walls of which does not exceed one millimetre. These are nicknamed eggshell ware. They have been found in the cavern lying near the village 'K a m a r e s' on the slopes of Ida, whence also their name "K a m a-r a i k a," |

#### HALL III

| | |
|---|---|
| 2000 - 1700 B. C. | Finds of Minoan civilization of the era of the ancient Minoan palace, excavated from the palace of Phaistos. |

**Show-case No. 41 :** The famous clay disk which is known as the "d i s k   o f   P h a i s t o s." Signs of a hieroglyphic script are still preserved on both of its sides, probably some script of a religious nature. The next has not yet been deciphered.

**Show-case NO. 34 :** Marvellous vessels of Kamares type from Phaistos.

## HALL   IV

**1700 - 1450  B. C.** Finds of Minoan civilization of the era of the new Minoan palaces, excavated from the palaces of Knossos, Phaistos and. Malia.

**Show-case No. 50 :** The two famous little idols of the Goddess of the snakes.

The larger of these idols represents the Goddess Mother. She has her hands extended with serpents crawling on them.

The smaller of the idols may represent the G o d d e s s   D a u g h t e r. She has her hands raised and holds in her palms some little serpents.

These idols were discovered in the sacred crypts of the western wing of the palace of Knossos.

**Show-case No. 51 :** The famous vessel used for libations–made of serpentine stone. It has the shape of a bull's head and is a masterpiece of Minoan art. The eyes of the head are of crystal and they attract much admiration, so natural are they and so brilliant. The bull, as we have said, was considered by the Minoans as a   s a c r e d   a n i m a l  and symbolized the force of impregnation.

This "r h y t o n" was found in the Little Palace.

**Show-case No. 56 :** The renowned "t a u r o k a t h a p t i s." This is a unique little idol made of ivory and represents a young bull-fighter making a dangerous acrobatic jump on the back of a bull.

This little idol is one of the most valuable exhibits of the museum. It is greatly admired as much for the 'motion' it imparts as for the articulate flexibility which the craftsman of those times was able to mould in the body.

55

Show-case No. 57 : A royal gaming board made of ivory, crystal, gold and other materials. It was found in the corridor of the palace of Knossos, whence the said corridor is known as the "C o r r i d o r  o f  t h e  D r a u g h t  B o a r d."

## HALL V

1450 - 1400 B.C.     Finds from the palace of Knossos of the Neo-palatial Minoan civilization.

Show-case No. 69 : Tablets of the Minoan script of the linear system. These tablets were i n v e n t o r i e s of various provisions or utensils. They have been found at Aghia Triada, Tylissos, Phaistos, and other places.

## HALL VI

1400 - 1350 B.C.     Finds at Knossos and Phaistos of Neo-palatial and Post-palatial Minoan civilization.

Show-case No. 87 : Gold ornaments from various parts of Crete, including the marvellous royal ring bearing the representation of a god.

## HALL VII

1700 - 1450 B.C.     Finds from different parts of Crete of the Neopalatial Minoan civilization.

Show-case No. 94 : The wonderful vase of the "h a r v e s t e r s  a n d  t h e w i n n o w e r s," which was used for libations. This is a masterpiece of Minoan art. It represents 'a group of men returning after moving the fields, singing and holding "s c y t h e s" as well as "w i n n o w s" for winnowing the corn. It was found in the villa of Aghia Triada.

Show-case No. 101 : The fine gold "J e w e l  o f  t h e  i n s e c t s," a sort of buckle or a clasp. It represents two bees facing one another and having between their feet a small round ball (honey). It was found in the tomb "K h r y s o l a k k o s" (golden pit or hole) near the Malia palace.

## HALL VIII

1700 - 1450 B.C.     Finds from the Zakros Palace of the Neo-palatial Minoan civilization.

Show-case No. 109 : A crystal vessel with a ring round its neck. It is ornamented with golden bands.

## HALL IX

1700 - 1450 B.C.    Finds from eastern Crete of the Neo-palatial Minoan civilization.

Show-case No. 121: A vase with a painted octopus. This is a masterpiece of Minoan art and it was found at Gournia.

## HALL X

1400 - 1100 B.C.    Finds of the post-palatial Minoan civilization.

## HALL XI

1100 - 800 B.C.    Finds of the Geometric civilization. Iron Age.

## HALL XII

800 - 650 B.C.    Finds from the Geometric and orientalising or Archaic periods.

## HALL XIII

This hall contains Minoan s a r c o p h a g i . These have the shape of a bath or chest. They were used for burying the dead, who were laid in a contracted position within. They have been found in various parts of Crete.

## HALL XIX

This hall contains works of art of the Archaic era from the VIIth to the VIth century B.C.

## HALL XX

Greek and Roman sculptures (5th century B.C. - 4th century A.D.

Show-case No. 145 : A 5th century B. C. gravestone with an archer from Aghia Pelagia ; the marble sarcophagus in front of the statue of Hadrian from near Iraklion : the 2nd century A.D. floor mosaic from Knossos with Posseidon riding sea horses.

Show-case No. 387 : The early Christian sarcophagus from Malia.

Show-cases Nos. 265, 266 : The two statues of Artemis shooting at one of the childtren of Niobe.


## First Floor of the Museum

### HALL XIV

Frescoes of the Minoan civilization.

At the northern side of the hall the visitor can see the  marvellous f r e s c o   o f   t h e   p r o c e s s i o n. It is estimated that it pictures some 400 figures and it has come from the 'corridor of the procession' of the Knossos Palace.

At the southern side one can admire the fresco of the Figure-of-Eight S h i e l d s (made originally from the hides of bulls). Such shields were used in war, and they come from the eastern wing of the Knossos palace.

In the same hall you can see the L a d i e s   i n   B l u e. These were either ladies of the aristocratic class or p r i e s t e s s e s. They were found in the eastern wing of the palace of Knossos.

In the same hall you can see the bas-relief on the 'P r i n c e   w i t h   t h e L i l i e s ' or the 'P r i e s t   K i n g.' One can see a copy of this bas-relief in the palace of Knossos.

Also in the same hall is the f r e s c o   o f   t h e   d o l p h i n s. This adorned the mansion of the queen in the eastern wing of the palace of Knossos where you can also see a copy of it.

The excellent fresco of the 'bull-fight' or 't a u r o m a c h i a' is also exhibited in this hall. This came from the eastern wing of the palace. As we mentioned before, these contests were a symbolic sacred nature.

Women as well as men participated in these contests. While it is a male who executes the dangerous jump on the back of the bull, two women are in position at the head and at the rear of the bull. The one makes ready to seize the jumping man ; the other swings in the air holding the horns of the bull ready to take her turn in executing the same kind of jump. Many of the taurokathaptes may have met their death at the deadly tips of the bull's horns.

Show-case No. 171 : In the middle of the hall the visitor can see an excellent s t o n e sarcophagus which was found at Aghia Triada. One side of this sarcophagus figures a bloody sacrifice of a bull made in honour of the dead king. Two other animals standing by are to be sacrificed. A procession of women follows. The other side figures a priestess wearing a crown on her head and carrying vessels.

The painting of these figures is very fine and the whole liturgy of sacrifice which they symbolize takes place to the sounds of the lyre.

Show-case No. 172 : This contains fragments of frescoes from the palace of Knossos.

## HALL XV

1600 - 1400 B.C.    Fresco finds from the Neo-palatial Minoan civilization.

Here is exhibited the famous fresco of the 'P a r i s i a n l a d y.' When excavated, Evans gave this fresco no other name in his great delight at the wonderful picture, so modern and so... pre-historic !

The 'Parisiana' depicts a priestess because she is wearing the "S a c r e d  K n o t" - the symbol of the deity. She was at the palace of Knossos.

## HALL XVI

1600 - 1400 B.C.    Fresco finds of the Neo-palatial Minoan civilization.

The visitor can see in this hall and on its western side the fresco of the C r o c u s - g a t h e r e r.

Evans interpreted this fresco as a figure of a boy. But in more recent studies, Professor N. P l a t o n, the archaeologist, proved that the figure represented is a monkey gathering crocuses ; these were plants which the Minoans used for making paints.

## HALL XVII

This hall contains the renowned 'Y a m a l a k i s  C o l l e c t i o n.'

Among the many exhibits one can distinguish in show-case No. 178 the 'K r i-
o p h o r o s' – a small bronze idol. This hall also contains beautiful seals
and other finds.

## HALL XVIII

This hall contains exhibits of Archaic, Classical, Hellenistic and Roman
handicrafts from the 7th up to the 1st century B.C.

In our present edition of this book we have included a reproduction of the palace of Knossos.

(Approved under Prot. No. 8907 of September
14, 1968 by the Directorate of Antiquities,
Section of Museums, of the Greek Ministry
of the Presidency of the State).

*Beautiful   Lady*

*Minoan dancer*

*Woman Toreador*

*Minoan Lady of snakes*

Μουσεῖον : Ἀκροβάτης ἐξ ἐλεφαντοστοῦν.
Museum : Ivory Acrobat.
Musée : Acrovat d'ivoire.
Museum : Akrobat aus Elfenbein.
Museo : Acrobata, In avorio.

Μουσεῖον : Ἡ σαρκοφάγος τῆς Ἁγ. Τριάδος.
Museum : Sarkophagus from Hagia Triada.
Musée : La Sarcophague de Hagia Triaeda
Museum : Sarkophag Ort Agia Trias
Museo : Il Sarcofago - di Hagia Triada.

Μουσεῖον : Οἱ Κυρίες μὲ τὰ γαλάζια, Τοιχογραφία.
Museum : Ladies in Blue, Fresco.
Musée : Les Dames en bleu, Fresque.
Museum : Die Damen in Blau, Fresko.
Museo : Le Singnore Azzurre, Affresco.

Μουσεῖον : Τὸ Ταυροκέφαλον Ρυτόν.
Museum : Bull's Head Rhyton.
Musée : Rhyton en tête de raureau.
Museum : Stierkopfrhyton.
Museo : Testa di toro - ritone.